RONALD
REAGAN

PRESIDENTIAL ◆ LEADERS

RONALD REAGAN

MICHAEL BENSON

LERNER PUBLICATIONS COMPANY / MINNEAPOLIS

For Anne Darrigan

Lerner Publications Company
A division of Lerner Publishing Group
241 First Avenue North
Minneapolis, MN 55401 U.S.A.

Website address: www.lernerbooks.com

Library of Congress Cataloging-in-Publication Data

Benson, Michael.
    Ronald Reagan / by Michael Benson.
        p.   cm. — (Presidential leaders)
    Includes bibliographical references and index.
    Summary: A biography of the fortieth president, who served from 1981–1989.
    ISBN: 0–8225–0815–X (lib. bdg. : alk. paper)
    1. Reagan, Ronald—Juvenile literature. 2. Presidents—United States—Biography—Juvenile
literature. [1. Reagan, Ronald. 2. Presidents.] I. Title. II. Series.
E877.B44   2004
973.927'092—dc21   2003008168

Manufactured in the United States of America
1 2 3 4 5 6 – JR – 09 08 07 06 05 04

CONTENTS

———— ✧ ————

As a teenager, Ronald "Dutch" Reagan worked as a lifeguard
because he liked helping people.

CHAPTER ONE

A DARING RESCUE!

*On August 3, 1928, we were wildly excited to see
"Life Guard Ronald 'Dutch' Reagan" mentioned
on the front page of the* Dixon Evening
Telegraph, *under an eighteen-point banner
headline: Pulled from the Jaws of Death.*

—Edmund Morris, *Dutch: A Memoir of Ronald
Reagan*

On August 2, 1928, seventeen-year-old Ronald Reagan
called to swimmers at Lowell Park in Dixon, Illinois, to
come out of the water. The sun was setting, and his duties
as a lifeguard had come to an end for the day. As soon as
the beach was empty, Reagan began closing up the bath-
house. Suddenly, he heard the sound of splashing water. He
ran to the edge of the Rock River and peered out across
the black water. In the twilight, he saw a shape splashing in
the water. A swimmer had failed to listen to Reagan's call
and was struggling against the strong current.

Without a moment's hesitation, Reagan ran into the water. Because the swift current could quickly carry him downstream, Reagan knew he could not swim straight toward the drowning man. He swam in a curve upriver, allowing the current to carry him to the swimmer. Reagan knew time was running out. The man had already slipped below the surface once before Reagan got to him.

The man panicked. He grabbed onto Reagan and began to pull him under. The two men struggled to stay afloat. Thinking quickly, Reagan had to punch the man into unconsciousness to make him stop squirming. He then wrapped his arm around the limp swimmer and began swimming back against the current. It took all of Reagan's strength to make it back to shore.

Reagan pulled the man out of the water. His boss, Mr. Graybill, was waiting for him at the water's edge and resuscitated the unconscious swimmer. The swimmer's narrow escape from death brought Reagan's number of rescues up to twenty-five.

Even at seventeen, Ronald Reagan's concern for people and for preserving life was strong. He displayed a determination to survive and to help others have full lives. Years later, Reagan carried these same qualities—with their strengths and weaknesses—into his two terms as president of the United States.

CHAPTER TWO

THE FAT LITTLE DUTCHMAN

[I remember] waiting and hoping for the winter freeze without snow so that we could go skating on the Rock River. . . . Swimming and picnics in the summer, the long thoughts of spring, the pain with the coloring of the falling leaves in autumn.

—Ronald Reagan, speaking of his childhood

Ronald Reagan was born on February 6, 1911, in an apartment above the local bank in Tampico, Illinois. According to family legend, Ronald's father took one look at his newborn son and said, "He looks like a fat little Dutchman. But who knows, he might grow up to be president someday." This comment earned Ronald the nickname "Dutch," which stuck with him for most of his youth.

Dutch's father, John Edward Reagan, was an Irish American. His family had moved to the United States from Ireland. The Reagans called John by his nickname, Jack.

Ronald Reagan (right) with brother John Neil in 1912. John preferred to be called by his middle name, Neil.

Politically, Jack was a Democrat who spoke passionately for the rights of the working man. He believed that all men were created equal.

Jack often put these beliefs into practice. When Dutch was young, a movie called *The Birth of a Nation* played at the local theater. Jack forbade anyone in his family to see the film because it glorified an organization called the Ku Klux Klan, which supported violence against African Americans.

On another occasion, when Jack checked into a hotel, the clerk looked at his Irish name and said, "You'll like it here, Mr. Reagan. We don't permit a Jew in the place." At this remark, Jack picked up his suitcase again. "I'm a Catholic," he fumed. "And if it's come to the point where you won't take Jews, you won't take me either."

Having refused to stay in the only hotel in town, Jack spent the night in his car.

According to Dutch, Jack Reagan was born to be a salesman. For much of his life, Jack worked at selling shoes. He eventually became part owner of his own store. Jack was popular with his customers. Dutch later wrote about his father, "He was endowed with the gift of blarney [flattery] and the charm of a leprechaun [a mythical Irish elf]."

Dutch's mother, Nelle Wilson Reagan, had a sweetness that often balanced the strong, practical attitudes of Jack's personality. Nelle worked as a community volunteer. She arranged readings for various ladies' societies and visited prisoners in the local jails.

———————— ✧

The Reagan family in 1914 (from left to right), Jack, Neil, Ronald, and Nelle. Reagan's haircut in this photo, called a Dutch boy, reinforced his family nickname, Dutch.

Nelle also visited a medical center for people sick with tuberculosis. Doctors often put people with this deadly lung disease in a special hospital. Most people avoided visiting tuberculosis clinics for fear that they might catch the disease. But Nelle wanted to help the sick people. The clinic became her favorite place to visit.

THE EARLY YEARS

Tampico was a quiet, country town. The Reagan house sat just across the street from the city park. Just beyond the park, trains chugged into and out of the town railroad station.

———————————— ✧ ————————————

A tuberculosis clinic in the early 1900s. Dutch's mother, Nelle, was a role model of compassion for him, visiting patients at clinics like this one.

Dutch once risked life and limb during a caper to swipe ice chips from an ice wagon like this one in his hometown of Tampico, Illinois.

────────────── ✧ ──────────────

Dutch could be a troublemaker at times. One afternoon, Dutch and his older brother Neil went exploring near the railroad station. They decided to sneak to the ice wagon and swipe some ice chips. The quickest route was to crawl beneath the train that was stopped at the station. The two boys had barely made it to the other side of the tracks when the train gave a heavy jerk forward and started to roll out. Had they been a moment slower, Dutch and Neil would have been crushed by the train wheels. Nelle watched the incident from the doorway of their home.

She stormed out to the ice wagon and pulled the boys home by their ears.

But Dutch also did many things to make his mother proud. Dutch learned to read before age five. Nelle always took time to read the boys stories each night. As she read, her finger followed the words. After a while, Dutch began to make a connection between the words Nelle spoke and the letters on the page. One night, Dutch sat down on the floor with the evening paper in front of him. When Jack asked him what he was doing, Dutch replied, "Reading." Jack then asked him to read something for him, which

Dutch Reagan (second row, first from left) *in his third-grade class photo. Dutch had learned to read before he entered school.*

Dutch did. Nelle was so proud she gathered the neighbors to listen to Dutch read the headline story from the paper.

By the time Dutch was eight years old, he had grown into an independent boy. He spent long afternoons exploring the woods outside of town with friends. He loved to hunt and fish.

But Dutch's life wasn't all carefree and fun. His family was not perfect. Dutch's father struggled with alcoholism. The young boy realized this when he was eleven years old. One snowy night, Dutch came home to find his father sprawled out on the front porch, his hair soaked with melting snow. Jack was too drunk to even stand up.

As Dutch bent down to grab hold of his father's coat, he could smell the sharp odor of whiskey on Jack's breath. Dutch then understood that his father was drunk. Somehow, Dutch managed to pull his father into the house and get him safely to bed. Within a few days, Jack returned to the hearty man Dutch knew and loved. But Dutch's image of his father changed. He realized that his father had flaws and personal challenges to overcome.

Nelle would remind Dutch and Neil that alcoholism was a sickness. She told them that they should never condemn Jack for something that was out of his control. Instead, she encouraged the boys to help their father and to love him.

To get a break from family duties, Nelle joined a theater group. Some days, Dutch would listen to his mother rehearse for local plays. She would recite classic speeches, dramatically weeping at tragic verses.

These dramas were Dutch's first introduction to acting and the theater. Nelle signed him up for children's plays.

Dutch often played small parts in Sunday school pageants. Once, draped with a sheet, he played the role of the Ghost of Christmas Yet to Come in Charles Dickens's *A Christmas Carol.* Although these productions pleased his mother, Dutch saw them more as a nuisance. He later wrote, "My own opinion is it had a somewhat stunting effect—since it took me away from my beloved sports."

CHAPTER THREE

BECOMING A FOOTBALL REGULAR

There was no field; no lines, no goal. Simply grass, the ball, and a mob of excited youngsters. . . . I worshiped the wild charge down the field and the final melee. . . . Those were the happiest times of my life.

—Ronald Reagan

When Dutch was nine, the family moved to Dixon, Illinois, ninety miles west of Chicago. Here he grew to love the local movie theater. He spent hours entranced by images of robbers, villains, and heroes flickering on the movie screen. During winter, Dutch went skating on the Rock River. He'd skate for miles against the wind, turn around and open his coat, and let the powerful gusts blow him back. Most important, in Dixon's schools, Dutch began his football career.

As a young boy, Dutch played football with neighborhood friends. They would gather at a town park to play football.

Dutch Reagan's family home in Dixon, Illinois. When Dutch wasn't at home, he could often be found playing football or at the movie theater.

They played without a field, lines, or goalposts—just a mob of excited young boys. One player would kick off, and the rest would start running, yelling, kicking, and eventually mounding into a pile of legs and arms.

HIGH SCHOOL FOOTBALL

Dutch entered high school in 1924. By this time, he was ready to play football in serious games—no more park pileups. But things beyond his control held Dutch back from being the star player he wanted to be. Although he didn't know it, Dutch was terribly nearsighted. Having lived with this problem his whole life, he figured it was the way all people saw. But Dutch learned otherwise one day when he was fourteen. Driving along in the family car,

Dutch noticed that his brother could read road signs that were just a blur to him. It suddenly occurred to Dutch that he had poor eyesight. He asked to borrow his mother's eyeglasses. Fitting them over his ears, Dutch saw the world in crisp view for the first time in his life. He was amazed that he could see separate leaves on the trees and clearly make out the hills on the horizon. Shortly after, Dutch got his own pair of glasses. Suddenly, catching a football became much easier for Dutch.

Dutch's size also stunted his football career. When he entered high school, he stood a mere five feet three inches tall. He weighed a puny 108 pounds. Most of the other players weighed at least forty pounds more. The football team did not even have pants small enough to fit him.

Dutch, about 1924. Despite a driving desire to play high school football, his poor eyesight and small size kept him from making the final cut his first year.

Dutch (bottom, center) *didn't give up on football. He attended practices to watch and support the squad until he made the team his junior year.*

✧ ————————————

Dutch didn't make the team his first year. But he still showed up at all the practices. He wanted to learn the fundamentals of the game for when he would be big enough to play.

Sure enough, Dutch grew quickly during high school. By his third year, he was big enough to line up with the rest of the team. Dutch's day came midseason that year. All week he had been learning plays at the guard position. On Saturday the coach read off the team's starting lineup. When he came to right guard, the coach followed with "Reagan." Dutch brimmed with excitement—his big moment had come. Dutch had a great game. For the rest of the year, he played at guard position, as a regular.

THE BEGINNINGS OF AN ACTOR

Dutch wasn't only growing up on the gridiron. He was also maturing in the classroom. During Dutch's junior year, Dixon's Northside High School hired a new English teacher. Mr. B. J. Frazer had a different approach to English composition. He announced to Dutch and the rest of his class that originality would be considered when grading essays. Up until this time, writing assignments were graded solely on spelling and grammar. Content was not considered.

This new approach forced Dutch to write more creatively. An average student in most subjects, Dutch soon discovered that he had a natural talent for writing. Before long, Mr. Frazer was asking Dutch to read his essays to the class. Dutch's first reading got a few laughs. This response encouraged Dutch, and soon he had the classroom roaring at his witty writings. Dutch learned that he enjoyed entertaining people and had a natural talent for it.

Spurred by his success in front of the class, Dutch decided to take his act a step further. That same junior year, he won his first part in a school play. The production was directed by Mr. Frazer. Teacher and student were becoming good friends. The play actor received enthusiastic praise. Dutch decided he really liked acting and tried out for another play. By his senior year, Dutch was in love with theatrical productions.

LIFEGUARD AT LOWELL

In the summer of 1926, Dutch took a job as a lifeguard at Lowell Park. He worked seven days a week, ten to twelve hours a day, watching swimmers in the Rock River. The section of river off Lowell Park was particularly difficult to swim. A dam downstream caused the current to quicken from time to time. Also, if a swimmer attempted to swim across the river to the other bank, he or she would have to be ready to go the entire 600 feet. Once started, there was no turning back. Dutch learned which spots were most dangerous and kept his eye on those areas.

During his lifeguard career, he saved seventy-seven people. Strangely enough, as Dutch remembers, not everyone appreciated the effort. He later wrote, "I got to recognize that people hate to be saved. Almost every one of them later sought me out and angrily denounced me for dragging them to shore. 'I would have been fine if you'd let me alone,' was their theme. 'You made a fool out of me trying to make a hero out of yourself.'"

Despite the ingratitude of some swimmers, the job paid well. By the time Dutch graduated in 1928, he had saved $400 for college. In those days, few people went to college. In fact, his brother Neil told him that going to college was a waste of time. But Dutch was determined to follow in the footsteps of one of Dixon's football heroes—star fullback Garland Waggoner. Waggoner went to Eureka College, about 110 miles southeast of Dixon. At Eureka, Waggoner had become an even bigger football star.

Despite his years of work as a summer lifeguard, Dutch did not have enough money saved for a full four years of college. Tuition alone was $180 a year. Room and board doubled the cost. All of Dutch's savings would be gone by the end of his first year. When Dutch visited the campus, he convinced the president and football coach to give him a Needy Student Scholarship. This grant covered half of his tuition. For Dutch, it was a start.

CHAPTER FOUR

FROM EUREKA TO RADIO

*A way of life was ending and it was hard for
me to see it as also a beginning.*
—Ronald Reagan, recalling graduation from Eureka
College, June 1932

At seventeen, Dutch began his freshman year at Eureka College. Over four years of high school, Dutch had reached a height of almost six feet one inch. He weighed a solid 175 pounds. Despite his size, however, Dutch spent his first season of college football on the bench. He did not have as much experience as the other players.

Yet a major event off the field placed Dutch in the limelight. As a small private school with only 250 students, Eureka was experiencing financial strains. In an effort to make ends meet, the new college president decided to lay off some faculty members and make other cuts. These cuts would keep many seniors from finishing the classes they needed to graduate. Despite the importance of the changes,

Reagan as member of the Eureka College football team in 1929. In addition to playing football, he was active in student and campus politics.

————————— ◇

neither the faculty nor the students had a say in what was going to be done. In fact, the cuts were to take place during the week when students went home for Thanksgiving vacation.

When students and faculty got wind of the plan, they were furious. A student committee was formed to discuss the possibility of calling a strike to stop the cuts from taking place. Dutch was elected to represent the freshmen on the committee. As a freshman, Dutch would be least affected by the cutbacks. This fact would make him an impartial party, or someone who spoke for everyone, not just for his own interests. After some debate, the committee selected him to represent the strike proposal to the student body.

Dutch reviewed the cutbacks and wrote a speech stressing how the cutbacks not only threatened the diplomas of graduating seniors but also the academic reputation of Eureka. In his speech, he pointed out that the students and faculty had been ignored in the decision. He detailed how the board had refused to listen to alternate ideas for saving money.

When Dutch delivered his speech, the students responded with shouts and cheers. Dutch later wrote, "For the first time in my life, I felt my words reach out and grab an audience, and it was exhilarating." At the end of his speech, the crowd rose to their feet with thunderous applause. The strike was approved.

Students held the strike as soon as they returned from Thanksgiving break. Instead of attending classes, most students stayed in their rooms and studied. The strike was a success. The school's leaders feared that they might have to close the college and were forced to reconsider their proposal. After a week, the new president resigned and the strike ended. Classes resumed as usual at Eureka College.

THE DAY IT RAINED

After Dutch's freshman year, he went back to his lifeguard job at Lowell Park. Over the summer, Dutch saved $200, but that was not enough money for a second year at Eureka. He decided against going back to school in the fall.

Luckily, Dutch had another option. One of his high school friends worked for a local surveyor. Surveyors study and document property boundaries. Dutch's friend talked him into applying for a job. The surveyor not only offered him the job but also offered Dutch a college scholarship.

After working for a year, the surveyor promised to pay his expenses at the University of Wisconsin. Dutch thought the offer was too good to pass up.

It rained on Dutch's first day of work. He and the rest of the crew were sent home. With nothing else to do, Dutch decided to take a car ride to the Eureka campus. The visit reminded him of the good times he'd had at Eureka.

Dutch found his football coach, Mac McKinszie, and told him he could not afford to attend Eureka another year. McKinszie was determined to help Dutch. Within a couple of hours, McKinszie had renewed his Needy Student Scholarship and arranged a job for Dutch, washing dishes at the girls' dormitory. Dutch called his mother to send him some clothes. He was staying at Eureka. "I've often wondered what might have happened to me if it hadn't been raining that day," Dutch later wrote.

Back on campus, Dutch threw himself into all arenas of college life. In addition to playing on the football team, he joined the swim team. His lifeguard

◇ ——————————

Reagan's lifeguard experience made him an exceptional addition to the Eureka College swim team. One of the best swimmers, he was team captain.

Reagan (second row, far right) poses with other members of the Eureka College drama club. Dutch received his first rave reviews while at Eureka.

───────────────── ✧ ─────────────────

experience paid off. He stood out as one of the top swimmers and became captain of the team. Dutch also participated in Eureka's drama program. He landed a role in the drama club's production of Edna St. Vincent Millay's *Aria da Capo.* The club performed the play in a national competition at Northwestern University in Chicago, Illinois. Dutch and other cast members gave a smashing performance. Eureka won second place in the contest, and Dutch received honorable mention for his portrayal of the shepherd Thyrsis. After the event, a faculty member at Northwestern told Dutch he should consider pursuing a career in acting. Dutch was thrilled by the suggestion.

Throughout his college years, Dutch was also involved in other student activities. He served as president of the Eureka Booster Club and spent two years on the yearbook editorial staff. He was elected to the student senate two years in a row. He served one year as student body president. Dutch graduated from Eureka in June 1932 with a degree in economics and sociology.

SPORTS BROADCASTER FROM WOC TO WHO

Dutch could have gone into business, but what he really wanted to do was entertain people. Six weeks after graduation, Dutch began visiting radio stations throughout Illinois in search of an announcer's job. The 1930s were the golden age of radio. In the decades before television, radio was America's favorite form of entertainment. Radio stations broadcast plays and shows to millions throughout the country. Radio programs held a certain magic. Performers used words and sounds to tell a story. The rest was up to the imagination of the audience. As Dutch described, "It was theater of the mind." The young graduate hoped to combine his love for sports with his gift for entertaining people. But first he needed to get his foot in the door. Dutch thought if he could land a job as a radio announcer, he could work his way up to a job as a sports broadcaster.

Lots of people were looking for jobs at radio stations, though. In the 1930s, the Great Depression was causing financial stress in homes and businesses across the United States. During this period of economic despair, thousands of businesses went bankrupt. Millions of people lost their jobs, savings, and homes. Finding an opening wouldn't be easy. After being turned down at numerous stations, Dutch found himself seated in front of Peter MacArthur, program director of WOC in Davenport, Iowa. Dutch began to tell MacArthur he'd take any job to get started in radio. "Where were you yesterday?" MacArthur interrupted. He had just hired someone the day before.

Dutch got up and walked out of MacArthur's office. On his way out, he mumbled, "How can you get to be a sports announcer if you can't even get a job at a radio station?" Dutch's words were just loud enough for MacArthur to hear. MacArthur asked Dutch if he knew anything about football. When Dutch told him that he'd played the game all his life, MacArthur gave him an audition.

For the tryout, Dutch stood in front of a microphone and announced a pretend game. He didn't have a script to work with. Dutch just made up plays as he went along. He chose to describe one of the games in which he'd played at Eureka. In this particular game, Eureka won the game in the last twenty seconds with a sixty-five-yard touchdown run.

"Here we are in the fourth quarter with Western State University leading Eureka College six to nothing," Dutch began. "Long blue shadows are settling over the field, and a chill wind is blowing through the end of the stadium." Eureka didn't have a stadium, but Dutch figured MacArthur wouldn't know that.

For fifteen minutes, Dutch described the teams running plays up and down the field. All the while, he was building up to the final touchdown. In the play, Dutch was at right guard. When the ball was snapped, he was supposed to put a block on the first player behind the defensive line. In the actual game, Dutch had completely missed his man. But during his audition, Reagan leveled a block on the player, freeing up the running back to score the game-winning touchdown. Dutch ended the broadcast with Eureka fans cheering. Pete gave Dutch a big smile and told him to be back on Saturday. He would be broadcasting one of the biggest matchups of the year, the 1932 Iowa-Minnesota college football game.

After the first game, Pete asked Dutch to broadcast Iowa's three remaining games of the season. Dutch hoped his play-by-play would land him a permanent job at WOC. By February 1933, Dutch was working as an announcer for $100 a month—a good salary in those hard times. Dutch announced commercials, radio programs, and other broadcasts. After three months in Davenport, Dutch was offered a position at WOC's sister station, WHO in Des Moines, Iowa.

———————————————————— ✧ ————————————————————

As an announcer for WHO Radio, Reagan once had to make up a description of an inning of a professional baseball game.

This was the big break he needed. At WHO, Dutch would be a full-time sports broadcaster.

Dutch spent the next four years at WHO. He broadcast numerous track events, football games, and baseball games. But Dutch didn't actually see many of the games he was describing. Instead, he relayed the events. From the press box at the field, a telegrapher would tap out the plays in Morse code and send them to the radio station. A telegram operator at the

Cardinals pitcher Dizzy Dean

────── ✧ ──────

station read the code and passed the information along to Dutch. Dutch then described the events to the audience. During one baseball game between the Chicago Cubs and the St. Louis Cardinals, Dutch was relaying the game. As usual, he received notes from the telegraph operator, describing the pitches. The telegraph operator passed him a note. But instead of the pitch, it read, "The wire's gone dead."

Thinking fast, Dutch had to stall until the line was fixed. Dutch continued broadcasting the game as if nothing was wrong. At the time, the game was scoreless in the ninth inning. The Cardinals' Dizzy Dean was on the mound facing the Cubs' Billy Jurges. Dutch slowly described the next pitch as a foul ball. Taking his time, Dutch announced another foul.

For seven long minutes, Dutch continued to call the game as if Jurges was fouling Dean's pitches. When the line was finally fixed, Dutch learned that Jurges had popped out at the first pitch. For days after the game, people stopped Dutch on the street and asked him if Jurges had set a record for foul balls.

JOINING THE CAVALRY

Outside the radio station, Dutch had many hobbies. One of his favorite pastimes was riding horses. Years earlier, during his lifeguard days, a man who lived near the river would sometimes take his horse for a ride in Lowell Park. Sometimes he let Dutch ride the horse. Later, in Des Moines, Dutch joined friends for horseback riding at a local stable.

Another announcer at WHO was a reserve officer in the army cavalry, or mounted troop division.

◇ ——————————

A sense of duty and a love for horses led Reagan to join the U.S. Cavalry reserves in 1937.

He told Dutch the Fourteenth Cavalry Regiment at Fort Des Moines offered young men an opportunity to become cavalry reserves. These soldiers served as backup soldiers for regular cavalry troops, to be called to duty in times of need. Dutch did not have a burning desire to become an army officer, but the program offered free training by some of the best cavalrymen in the country—and unlimited use of the horses. This deal was too good to pass up. Dutch joined the cavalry unit in 1937. He quickly became a second lieutenant of the Army Officers Reserve Corps of the Cavalry.

With a reserve officer's commission, a good career, and a growing following of fans, Dutch Reagan seemed to have it all. But his rise to fame was only beginning. His next step would put him in an even bigger spotlight.

CHAPTER FIVE

THE MAKINGS OF A STAR

*I took my place on the set, the lights went on,
and the director said, "Camera ... Action!"
Suddenly, my jitters were gone. ... I forgot all
about the camera and the lights and the crew
and concentrated on delivering my lines in a way
that I hoped would make B. J. Frazer proud.*

—Ronald Reagan, recalling the filming of his first
movie, *Love Is on the Air*

Since his high school theater productions, Dutch had loved
acting. His work at WHO improved his skills, forcing him
to be theatrical and entertaining through words alone. As
chance would have it, Dutch's job at WHO helped lead
him to an acting career in another way—by sending him
to Hollywood. Each year, the Cubs team held its preseason
spring training on Catalina, an island off the coast of
southern California. Starting in 1935, Dutch traveled there
to cover the training camp.

The call of Hollywood was too much for the actor in Reagan to resist while on assignment in California for WHO Radio in 1937. He visited a Hollywood studio and met with an actors' agent.

———————————— ✧ ————————————

Catalina was only a boat ride away from Hollywood, the movie capital of the world. One day in 1937, Dutch decided to skip out on spring training and take a trip to a Hollywood studio. After touring a studio that afternoon, Dutch stopped by a nightclub to visit a friend, Joy Hodges. Joy was a singer who had moved to Los Angeles hoping to break into the movies. She had won several small parts and worked nights singing at the club. Dutch told Joy about his desire to become an actor. Joy knew an agent who could honestly tell Dutch if he had any talent. She set up a meeting between the two men.

GOD MADE ONLY ONE ROBERT TAYLOR

At ten o'clock the next morning, Dutch met with agent Bill Meiklejohn. Meiklejohn asked Dutch about his acting experience. Dutch lied a little to make himself look good.

He described the Eureka Dramatic Club as a professional acting company. He also told the agent that he earned double what he actually did. Finally, Dutch said, "Look, Joy told me that you would level with me. Should I go back to Des Moines and forget this, or what do I do?"

Meiklejohn did not answer but picked up the phone and dialed Warner Brothers studio—one of Hollywood's biggest movie studios. He asked for Max Arnow, an important and powerful casting director. When Arnow got on the other line, Bill told him, "I have another Robert Taylor sitting in my office." Taylor was a popular young actor with uncommonly good looks. Dutch could hear Arnow on the other end of the phone reply, "God made only one Robert Taylor!"

Still, Meiklejohn convinced Arnow to see Dutch in person. Arnow was impressed by the young man's good looks and easy charm. He scheduled a screen test. In screen tests, actors auditioned for the camera to see how they looked on film. For his test, Dutch exchanged a few lines from a popular film called *The Philadelphia Story* with an actress. Meiklejohn then told Dutch to expect a call in a few days. Dutch simply replied that he would be on a train to Des Moines tomorrow. He had a Cubs game to broadcast. Meiklejohn and Arnow could not believe Dutch wouldn't postpone his trip back to Iowa. As Dutch left California, he wondered if he had been a fool to take that train.

Less than forty-eight hours after the train pulled into Des Moines, Dutch got a telegram from Meiklejohn. It read: "Warners offers contract. Seven years—one year option—starting $200 a week—what shall I do?" Dutch hurried to the telegraph office and wrote his reply: "Sign before they can change their minds—Dutch Reagan."

Reagan's early glamour shot following his Hollywood transformation from Dutch to Ronald Reagan

GOOD-BYE DUTCH, HELLO RONALD

A month after Dutch signed on with Warner Brothers, he said good-bye to his friends in Des Moines. Dutch took off for California with $600 in his pocket and everything he owned packed into his convertible. "With the top of my car open to the wind and the sun shining on my head," Dutch recalled, "[that trip] was one of the highest highs. I was on my way to Hollywood."

Within a few days, Dutch was dragged through a series of changes—new hairstyle, new wardrobe, and even a new name. Dutch Reagan just didn't sound like a movie star's name. Arnow wanted to choose a name that fit Reagan's handsome, suave appearance. Arnow and several Warner Brothers press agents sat around a table staring at Dutch. They fired suggestions back and forth. Dutch had never really liked his given name. He much preferred to be called by his nickname. But he asked how "Ronald Reagan" sounded.

The agents decided that wasn't so bad, and it was Ronald Reagan from that point on.

IN THE MOVIES

For his first movie, *Love Is on the Air,* Reagan played a familiar role—a radio announcer. His character hosted a popular radio show. Through his radio show, Reagan's character uncovers shady schemes in local politics. The young actor received positive reviews. *The Hollywood Reporter,* an important movie paper, wrote: *"Love Is on the Air* presents a new leading man, Ronald Reagan, who is a natural, giving one of the best first picture performances Hollywood has offered in many a day."

Reagan appeared in eight movies during his first year at Warner Brothers. In those days, actors were sometimes required to supply their own wardrobe. Reagan only owned

——————————— ✧ ———————————

A scene from Swing Your Lady, *1938. The film was one of eight in which Reagan (far right) acted during his first year with Warner Brothers.*

Reagan adds air to the tire of coactor Jane Wyman. Reagan and Wyman quickly became a "Hollywood item," dating extensively.

four suits, and he often wondered how he would manage a script with eight or more wardrobe changes. Near the end of a film, Reagan would wear a suit that he had worn in earlier scenes, hoping the audience would not notice.

Before long, Reagan began to make money in his acting career. Soon after his first successful Hollywood pictures, Reagan asked Nelle and Jack to move to California. He bought them a house in southern California—the first house his parents had ever owned. Reagan made Jack president of his fan club.

In 1938 Reagan starred in the comedy *Brother Rat*, playing a cadet at a military academy. Also appearing in the film was a lovely, twenty-five-year-old actress, Jane Wyman. A romantic relationship quickly grew between the two Hollywood stars.

Warner Brothers decided to use the romance to build up publicity for the movie. They sent Reagan and Wyman on a tour, performing a musical variety show. As the couple traveled across the country, famous gossip columnist Louella Parsons accompanied them. She printed items about the Reagan-and-Wyman romance daily.

Brother Rat was a hit, and so were Ronald and Jane. On January 26, 1940, Reagan and Wyman were married.

JANE WYMAN

Jane Wyman was born on January 4, 1914, as Sarah Jane Fulks. Like Reagan, she began her show business career in radio—as singer Jane Durrell. She changed her name to Jane Wyman in the 1930s, after a few leading film roles.

Wyman's popularity as a film star grew during the 1940s. Her performance as the girlfriend of an alcoholic in *The Lost*

Weekend (1945) earned the respect of film critics. In 1948 Wyman won an Academy Award for her performance as a deaf mute in *Johnny Belinda*. During her career, she was nominated for three more Academy Awards.

By 1960 Wyman had retired from the big screen. She made a comeback to television in 1981. From 1981 to 1990, Wyman starred as Angela Channing in the CBS primetime soap opera *Falcon Crest*.

Reagan as the Gipper

Shortly after the wedding, the couple bought a house in Hollywood.

WIN ONE FOR THE GIPPER

In 1940 Warner Brothers announced plans to make a movie about the life of legendary University of Notre Dame football coach Knute Rockne. Reagan desperately wanted to play the part of George Gipp—a star football player who becomes fatally ill. To win the role, Reagan cluttered the producer's desk with photos of himself at Eureka, suited up in his football uniform. His relentless approach worked. Reagan got the part.

The movie, *Knute Rockne—All American,* was a great success. Reagan received praise for his portrayal of "the Gipper." He gripped the hearts of America in Gipper's deathbed scene. As the Gipper lay dying, he tells Knute Rockne (played by Pat O'Brien), "Go out and win one for the Gipper."

Proud parents Ronald and Jane with their baby daughter, Maureen, in 1941. Reagan's career began to take off that same year.

Reagan's performance as the Gipper would become his most remembered role.

WHERE'S THE REST OF ME?

The year 1941 would also be memorable for Ronald and Jane. On January 4, Wyman gave birth to their daughter, Maureen.

Reagan's life was moving fast. His career was really picking up speed. In 1941 Reagan landed another big role, this time as a leading character. The picture was called *King's Row*. Reagan played the part of Drake McHugh, a smooth talker with the ladies.

Reagan's key scene was to be played in bed. An accident in the railroad yards injures Drake. The hospital doctor disapproves of Drake dating his daughter and decides to punish him for it. When Drake regains consciousness, he discovers that the doctor has amputated both of his legs. Reagan had only one line—five words—with which to portray the shock and horror of this realization.

The scene haunted Reagan for weeks. He continually practiced the line in front of the mirror, in the car while driving to and from the studio, and in corners of the studio. He wanted the horror of his discovery to seem genuine. When the day of the shoot finally came, he was ready.

The stage designers had created a bed with a hole in the mattress. Reagan would kneel on a box inside the hole, hiding his legs from viewers. Then he would be covered with a sheet, creating the illusion that his legs had been cut off. Reagan stepped into the hole cut in the mattress. He spent an hour in the confined bed. He thought about his torso and the flat sheets below it where his legs should have been.

By the time Reagan heard the director's voice yell "Action!" he was completely absorbed in his role. Slowly, in a daze, he opened his eyes and looked around. Gradually, his gaze traveled downward, and he tried to reach where his legs should have been. "Randy!" he screamed to another character. The actress playing Randy appeared at his side. Drake looked up and cried, "Where's the rest of me?" There was no need to shoot the scene twice. Reagan gave a perfect delivery the first time.

King's Row was a hit. Movie critics especially praised Reagan's convincing performance. Yet despite his success, Reagan was not fulfilled. The question "Where is the rest of me?" was a question the actor was asking himself.

He believed there was more to life than just acting. As an actor, he felt his life consisted of pretending day after day. He wanted to do something more meaningful. The thirty-four-year-old actor began to think about the three loves in his life: drama, politics, and sports. Acting in films felt like less and less of a challenge, and he could no longer be a top football player. But his potential in politics had yet to be realized. By the end of the year, Reagan would find himself and his country swept up in events that would change the world.

WORLD WAR II

On December 7, 1941, Japanese planes attacked the U.S. Naval Base at Pearl Harbor, in the Hawaiian Islands. The surprise attack killed 2,300 Americans and sank five U.S. battleships. The event brought the United States into World War II, a massive global conflict in which

——————— ✧
Reagan served with the Motion Picture Army Unit during World War II (1939–1945), earning the rank of captain.

the United States, Great Britain, and their allies fought Japan, Germany, and their allies.

As a member of the army cavalry reserves, Reagan was called into active duty. He was stationed at a base near San Francisco as part of a cavalry unit.

Reagan's poor eyesight kept him away from being called overseas to fight in combat. Instead, he was assigned to the Motion Picture Army Unit in Culver City, California. Reagan helped make training films and movies designed to boost the morale of the troops and citizens. Another one of Reagan's jobs was to prepare films about the progress of the war for military leaders in Washington. This included ghastly war footage that was considered too horrible to be seen by the general public. He served in this job until his discharge after the war ended in 1945.

Back at home, Reagan's life got a little busier. He and Jane decided to adopt a son, whom they named Michael Edward. Reagan once again became active in the film industry. Over the years, he had made many good friends in the business. Many of these people had been impressed with his leadership abilities, the same leadership he had shown at Eureka College. In 1947 he was elected president of the Screen Actors Guild (SAG). This organization protected the rights of actors and settled disputes between actors and movie studios. As guild president, Reagan worked on behalf of actors, making sure they received fair treatment and fair pay.

CHAPTER SIX

RISING IN POLITICS

I realized that the real enemy wasn't big business, it was big government.

—Ronald Reagan, referring to his emerging political philosophy

Reagan's role as SAG president placed him at the forefront of an important legal battle affecting the film industry. After the war, a private chain of movie theaters filed a lawsuit against movie studios. At this time, studios not only produced films but also owned most of the theaters where they were shown. Smaller theaters not owned by the studios struggled to draw an audience. Owners of these theaters felt studios created a monopoly—meaning they controlled all of the theater business. Monopolies were illegal because they did not allow fair competition. In a major legal decision, the Supreme Court ruled that movie studios could either make pictures or operate theaters, but they could not do both.

Reagan (third from right) *with other members of the Screen Actors Guild. As SAG president, Reagan advocated for actors' interests.*

Reagan disagreed with the Supreme Court's ruling. He felt that although the system was tough on smaller theaters, a fierce competition existed among the different movie studios themselves. Because of this competition, there was no monopoly. No single studio controlled the movie industry. In fact, Reagan felt the competition was good for the movie industry. It forced studios to make higher quality movies.

Before the war, Reagan had been a firm Democrat, just like his father. But Democrats supported the breakup of big businesses. After the movie studio decision, Reagan began to question the views of the Democratic Party.

In the late 1940s, Jane's acting career began to take off while Reagan's movie career was grinding to a halt. Their days as a happy pair were also coming to an end. The couple discussed divorce, and Jane finally filed for it. At a time when joint custody was virtually nonexistent, Jane won custody of their children, though Reagan was able to visit them on weekends. Jane had two other marriages after her divorce with Reagan.

THREAT OF COMMUNISM

Reagan's interest and involvement in politics continued to grow throughout the 1950s. His political rise came about during an era when many Americans were concerned about the future of their country and the world. In particular, the U.S. public was concerned about the spread of Communism.

Communism is a form of government in which the state owns almost all property. The largest and most powerful Communist nation at the time was the Soviet Union, a group of states controlled by Russia. In the Soviet Union, the government owned most of the factories, farms, and businesses. Citizens worked for little or no wages, but their basic necessities such as food and shelter were provided by the government. This was a direct contrast to the American economic system of capitalism. In capitalist societies, private individuals and businesses, not the states, own most of the property. People work for wages, which they use to buy things.

The Soviet Union and other Communist nations differed from the United States in another crucial way. The United States was a democracy, where citizens had the right to choose their leaders. They also enjoyed the freedom to think, speak, and write about their political beliefs without being punished by the government. This was not the case in the Soviet Union. Soviet citizens did not choose their leaders. And those who questioned their rulers risked imprisonment or even execution.

Relations between the United States and the Soviet Union had been hostile since the Soviet Union became a Communist country in the early 1900s. During World War II, the two nations had fought side-by-side against Japan, Germany, and their allies. But following the war, relations between the two countries became unfriendly again. At war's end, the Soviet Union took control of its eastern European neighbors. It installed Communist governments in these countries and limited the freedoms of their citizens. These actions alarmed the United States and its allies, which included a number of democracies in Western Europe, such as Great Britain and France.

By the end of the 1940s, most of the world had become divided between the Western democracies, led by the United States, and the eastern Communist group, or bloc, controlled by the Soviet Union. The hostility between democracies and the bloc nations came to be known as the Cold War. Although the two sides never fought one another directly, their chilly relations had a major impact on world politics. Each side accused the other of trying to dominate the world.

Many Americans feared that the Soviet Union was secretly trying to overthrow the U.S. government. They worried that Communists were working in the government and plotting to take over. This period in the 1950s came to be known as the Red Scare—red was the main color of the Soviet flag—as a wave of fear swept the country. Some U.S. leaders also claimed that Communists controlled the movie business.

Senator Joseph McCarthy (seated, left) and other members of the House Committee on Un-American Activities in 1950. This congressional committee sought to stamp out Communism in the United States during the Red Scare.

They investigated these claims. Those who were suspected of being Communists were blacklisted. This meant they were forbidden to work in the industry.

MEETING NANCY

One morning in 1951, Reagan received a call from movie director Mervyn LeRoy. LeRoy explained that an actress working on one of his pictures was quite upset. Apparently, this woman, Nancy Davis, was listed as a member of several Communist groups. As a result, she was receiving meeting notices in the mail. But Davis did not belong to any Communist group. She worried that her career might be damaged if word of this situation got out to the public. As president of the Screen Actors Guild, Reagan had been working against Communist groups in the film industry, so he seemed the likely person to contact.

Reagan did some research. He found that there was more than one Nancy Davis connected with show business. After only a few minutes of research, he concluded that LeRoy's Nancy Davis was not connected to any Communist group. He called LeRoy with the news that she was cleared.

Before long, LeRoy called Reagan back. Apparently, the message was not enough to satisfy Davis. "She's a worrier," LeRoy said. "She's still worried that people are going to think she's a Communist. Why don't you give her a call?" Reagan agreed to take Davis to dinner and explain the whole story to her in person.

Over dinner, Davis at first fumed about the whole situation. But soon the conversation turned to other topics. They exchanged stories about their lives and found out they got along really well. Reagan did not want the evening to end. He asked Davis if she'd like to go to a club down the street.

——————————— ✧

As an anti-Communist and president of the Screen Actors Guild, Reagan held sway with the U.S. government. Here Reagan testifies before the House Committee on Un-American Activities.

He brought her home at three in the morning and asked her if she'd like to go to dinner the following evening. She accepted.

Reagan and Davis dated often for the next several months. After a while, Reagan realized that Davis was the only woman he wanted to take out. One night over dinner, he said, "Let's get married."

Davis's hazel eyes looked into Reagan's, and she answered, "Let's."

Reagan knew if the press learned about their wedding plans, reporters would storm the church. He suggested they have a small, quiet wedding. Davis agreed with the plan. In a little church in California's San Fernando Valley, Reagan and Nancy were married on March 4, 1952. Less than a year later, their first child, Patricia Ann, was born.

Ronald Reagan and Nancy Davis pose for the cameras during a dinner date in 1952. The couple's romance quickly led to marriage.

The Reagans, Ronald and Nancy, on their wedding day, March 4, 1952
──────────── ✧

Yet while Reagan's home life was on the upswing, his movie career took a downward turn. Reagan was only being offered roles in low-quality pictures. Reagan and Nancy decided that he would not accept roles in bad pictures. Instead, he would hold out for something really good. Studios continued to send Reagan scripts, but none of them appealed to him.

SPOKESPERSON FOR GE

By the early 1950s, a new form of entertainment was sweeping across the nation—television. Many Hollywood stars were switching from film to television. Reagan had never wanted to do a television series. In his opinion, it was the "professional kiss of death" to a movie star. At the time, movie theater owners thought no one would pay for a ticket to see someone they could see at home on TV.

Also, most TV series ended after two or three years. Even after that short time, audiences and producers tended to see an actor only as the character he or she played on TV. Once they were typecast in this way, it was difficult to find other roles in the future.

Yet Reagan needed a job to support his new family. In 1954 Taft Schreiber, a television executive, called Reagan with a proposal. In those days, television programs were sponsored, or paid for, by a single company. The television program was often named after the company, such as *Kraft Television Theater* and *Coke Time*. The General Electric Company (GE) was in the market for a new program to sponsor. Schreiber proposed a weekly dramatic program in which Reagan would serve as the host. He would also act a few times a season. Reagan thought being a host would save him from being typecast. The idea also offered him

✧ ———————————
Reagan as host of the popular General Electric Theater *television program*

an opportunity to share in the growing prosperity of television (a period later known as the Golden Age of Television). Reagan accepted the proposal. Every Sunday, Reagan hosted the *General Electric Theater,* which offered a different story each week. Many of Hollywood's finest actors appeared in these GE plays.

In addition to being host of the TV series, General Electric's chairman asked Reagan to travel to GE plants around the country to help boost employee spirits. He wanted to make sure his employees were happy at their jobs. At first, Reagan simply walked down assembly aisles and occasionally talked to small groups of employees. But after a couple years, GE asked Reagan to speak to employees who were working on a charity fund-raising project. Reagan gave a speech about pride in giving and the importance of doing things to help others instead of waiting for the government to do it. His speech received a huge ovation. Surprised, the GE representative with him said, "I didn't know you could give speeches." To which Reagan replied, "I have been doing that for quite a while."

From that point on, Reagan became a popular speaker. The company soon asked Reagan to speak to large groups of GE employees and clients. He also spoke at business conventions and to other groups. Many of Reagan's speeches focused on the role of government in businesses. While speaking to other organizations, Reagan still traveled around the country visiting GE plants. In eight years, he visited each of the company's 139 plants at least once. He met more than 250,000 employees. These experiences gave Reagan a chance to sharpen his speaking skills. It also gave him the opportunity to carry his political views to a growing audience.

And Reagan's views were changing as his experiences with government and business changed him.

Reagan's family was also experiencing changes. On May 28, 1958, Nancy gave birth to a boy, Ronald Prescott.

FROM DEMOCRAT TO REPUBLICAN

Throughout the 1950s and into the 1960s, Reagan's beliefs drifted further away from the policies of the Democratic Party. In his younger years, Reagan had seen the Democrats as supporters of the working people. In the 1930s, Democratic president Franklin D. Roosevelt had sponsored programs to help ordinary Americans during the Great Depression. But these programs had led to high taxes. Some Americans saw high taxes as a burden on businesses and on taxpayers. From their point of view, people and businesses that were heavily taxed had less money to spend and invest. These Americans further believed that the situation was bad for the economy as a whole.

In the 1940s, Reagan himself experienced the burden of high taxes. He was very well paid as an actor. But most of his earnings—90 percent of his salary—went to the government as taxes. To Reagan, this seemed unfair. He also felt it was bad for business. He questioned why he should work when nearly all his earnings wound up in the hands of the government.

In 1952 and 1956, in contrast to previous presidential elections, Reagan had campaigned for the Republican candidate, Dwight D. Eisenhower. Yet Reagan remained a Democrat. But as he spent more time touring the country and meeting with business leaders, Reagan sided more and more with an approach that supported lower taxes.

Reagan believed this approach would help everyone. Lower taxes would mean more profitable businesses. More profitable businesses would hire more employees and pay them better wages. The Republican Party was leading the call for this kind of tax policy.

In 1960 Reagan campaigned for Richard Nixon during Nixon's unsuccessful presidential campaign. Reagan also gave speeches for Nixon during Nixon's run for California governor in 1962. During the campaign, Reagan made his party switch official at a Republican fund-raiser. While he was speaking, a woman in the audience stood up and asked him if he had registered as a Republican. Reagan replied, "Well no, I haven't yet. But I intend to."

"I'm a registrar," she said. The woman then walked down the center aisle and placed a registration form in front of Reagan. He signed it and became a Republican. Reagan straightened up and said to the audience, "Now, where was I?"

Ronald Reagan's political transformation was complete. But his political career was only just beginning.

CHAPTER SEVEN

GOVERNOR REAGAN

You and I have the ability and the dignity and the right to make our own decisions and determine our own destiny. . . .

—Ronald Reagan, during an NBC televised speech on behalf of Republican presidential candidate Barry Goldwater, 1964

During the 1964 presidential election, Reagan made a televised speech on behalf of Republican candidate Barry Goldwater. Although Goldwater lost the presidential election in a landslide to Democrat Lyndon Johnson, Reagan's speech received rave reviews. California Republicans saw Reagan as a potential candidate for governor. The Republican nominee would face a stiff test against Democrat Pat Brown, who was running for a third term as governor. Republicans asked Reagan to run against Brown in the 1966 election.

At first, Reagan turned down their offer. He promised to campaign hard for whomever the party chose as a candidate, but he was not interested in the job. In his early fifties at the time, Reagan figured he was too old to consider a new career. But Republicans continued to encourage him to run. Reagan thought his mind was set, but then he began to worry about the future of the Republicans in California. Could he do something to help?

Reagan decided to go on a speaking tour for six months. He figured that in six months' time he could find a suitable candidate to run for governor instead of him. Instead of finding a candidate, Reagan continually heard people ask him to run for governor. At the end of six months, Reagan asked Nancy, "How do you say no to all these people?" They decided the best thing to do was run. On a television broadcast on January 4, 1966, Reagan announced his decision to seek the Republican nomination for governor. After decades of campaigning for other candidates, Ronald Reagan was finally promoting himself for office.

WHO KILLED ABE LINCOLN?

After winning the Republican nomination, Reagan quickly learned that he would be in for a rough battle. Pat Brown continually brought up Reagan's career as an actor, stating that he had no experience in the political arena. "Reagan has never held any political office before and here he is seeking the top spot in the government of California," Brown declared.

Reagan knew he needed to handle the situation carefully. A great number of people had certain beliefs about actors. Some people felt that since actors spend a majority of their life pretending, that's all they are capable of doing.

Reagan and Pat Brown debate in 1966. In a bold political move,
Reagan invited citizens' questions during debates.

────────────────── ✧ ──────────────────

Could anyone who spent decades pretending to be other
people be anything more than a fake? Could he be genuine?
Reagan could only work hard to get his message across and
show people he was more than just an actor.

Another strike Brown made against Reagan was accusing
him of not writing his own speeches. But Reagan did in
fact write his own speeches. Yet simply saying so would not
be enough to convince the public. He needed to prove that
his speeches were his own thoughts. He decided that
instead of making speeches, he could say a few words to
the audience and then allow questions. Reagan's political
professionals were concerned about this approach. They
were worried Reagan might look foolish if he answered a
question in the wrong way. Reagan commented, "They
were used to hiding candidates, not turning them loose."

Reagan and his political professionals decided they needed to take a chance if they wanted to prove their candidate was more than just an actor. Reagan was allowed to interact with the audience. The plan worked wonderfully. Reagan proved to be intelligent and genuinely interested in the thoughts of the people. And the open format also gave him a chance to learn about the issues on the minds of Californians.

Reagan's new strategy did not cause Governor Brown to change his strategy. He continued to attack Reagan's acting career. Late in the campaign, Brown made a fatal move. He appeared in a television commercial in which he asked a group of children, "I'm running against an actor, and you know who killed Abe Lincoln, don't you?" Most people felt comparing Reagan to assassin John Wilkes Booth—the actor who had murdered President Lincoln—was unfair and distasteful. On Election Day, November 8, 1966,

The Reagans emerge from voting booths on Election Day, 1966.

Reagan defeated Governor Brown, winning 58 percent of the votes.

Reagan assigned some of the best businesspeople in the United States to his administration. He stood aside and let these experts do their jobs. Reagan then made final policy decisions based on the advice of his experts. Some people criticized Reagan for his hands-off approach to management. But Reagan believed that the cornerstone to good management was to set clear goals and then appoint good people to help achieve them.

Reagan's first task as governor was to fix the state budget. California was spending one million dollars more each year than it was taking in. The state's budget deficit had been a key campaign issue, and Reagan vowed to squeeze and cut until the state of California was back in financial order.

By the end of the first year, Reagan's team had reduced the state's spending dramatically. But it was not enough to cover the deficit left by Brown's administration. Reagan was forced to ask for a tax increase.

Reagan did not want to increase taxes. In his campaign, he had called for lower taxes. His opponents criticized him for changing course. But Reagan assured Californians that he would refund some of their money to them as soon as he could.

EQUAL OPPORTUNITY

As governor, Reagan wanted to learn all he could about the concerns of California's citizens. Reagan visited African American neighborhoods in Sacramento. He disguised himself to avoid reporters and visited families in these neighborhoods. He wanted to learn what was on their minds.

One thing Reagan discovered was that African Americans believed they were not being fairly considered for state government jobs. Reagan looked into this complaint. He found out that the only state jobs held by African Americans were janitorial positions. Civil service tests were designed to keep African Americans out of higher-paying jobs. In one case, Reagan discovered that applications had been thrown away by state employment workers because a few questions had been left blank. When Reagan later met with Sacramento officials, he instructed them not to throw away applications. He also demanded they hire more minorities for state jobs.

Reagan also visited the Mexican American barrio (neighborhood) in East Los Angeles. Families in this neighborhood expressed concern about education. One mother told Reagan that her son had difficulty in school because he had problems speaking English. The boy's teacher thought the child was developmentally disabled and sent him to a class for developmentally disabled children. Luckily, another teacher realized the problem and took him out of the class. The boy graduated from high school with the highest honors. This mother knew that other children were not as lucky. Reagan suggested that a group of mothers take turns visiting their children's classroom to monitor their schooling. They said they'd be happy to do that, but only people with teaching certificates were allowed to participate in the classroom.

Reagan thought it was crazy that parents could not be directly involved in their child's education. He believed parents should be a bigger part of the school system. He took steps to change this approach to education.

Reagan's interest in educational policies inspired California schools to develop a program that supported parent involvement in their children's education.

RIOTS ON BERKELEY CAMPUS

In 1965 America began fighting in a war against North Vietnam. North Vietnamese leader Ho Chi Minh wanted to unite North and South Vietnam under a Communist government. In an effort to protect Southeast Asia from the spread of Communism, President Lyndon Johnson sent U.S. troops to fight the Communists. The war quickly became costly in terms of money and American lives. Although U.S. forces won the major battles, the Vietnamese Communists would not give up the fight. To many, it seemed a war America could not win. As the war became more and more costly, many Americans questioned U.S. involvement.

U.S. troops go into action in Vietnam.

Antiwar protests grew in response to U.S. involvement in Vietnam. Many of these protests happened at the University of California at Berkeley (above) while Reagan was governor of that state.

⎯⎯⎯⎯⎯⎯⎯⎯⎯⎯⎯ ◇ ⎯⎯⎯⎯⎯⎯⎯⎯⎯⎯⎯

During the 1960s, there were many demonstrations— large gatherings of people showing support for an issue—on California's college campuses. Many of these demonstrations were protests against the Vietnam War. Such demonstrations are a legal right under the U.S. Constitution. They are part of every U.S. citizen's right to free speech.

Student protesters opposed not just the war but also the draft. The draft was a system in which the government required all able-bodied men to be available for military service. Men who were drafted might be required to serve in the army and possibly be sent to fight in Vietnam. For some Americans, the idea of being forced to fight, and possibly die, in a war that they opposed was unfair. Millions of Americans spoke out against the war and the draft.

Governor Reagan assures reporters and Californians that he has demonstrators at Berkeley under control.

——————————————— ✧ ———————————————

Some radical protesters, however, thought speech was not enough. These people turned to violence to try to make their point. During an eleven-month period in the late 1960s, eight bombings and attempted bombings occurred at the University of California's Berkeley campus. During that same period, police took more than two hundred rifles, pistols, and shotguns from students. They also collected almost one thousand sticks of dynamite and dozens of gasoline bombs.

Reagan met with students and discussed the issues to try to calm the situation. At one meeting, the students' spokesman told the governor that the students wanted to talk to him but that he could never understand them. But Reagan did try to understand the students' position.

When he was seventeen years old, he, too, had been involved in campus protests. But those protests had been much different from the ones at Berkeley. These stakes were much higher. The Berkeley students weren't protesting against job cuts. They were opposing a controversial war and the draft, and the protests often became violent. Still, Reagan believed the students had a right to express their grievances, but they had to do so peacefully.

In 1968 the university purchased some land on which they planned to build dormitories. But the dirt lot stood empty, and people began to use it as a parking lot. In April 1969, the *Berkeley Barb* community newspaper ran a headline reading, "Bring shovels, hoses, flowers, soil, colorful smiles, laughter, and lots of sweat." The people planned to transform the lot into a park.

The following Sunday, hundreds of people showed up to work, including faculty members and their families, townspeople, and students. They planted grass, trees, and flowers. They even built a playground. For several weekends, thousands of people came to People's Park to plant, work, and play.

When university officials found out about the park, they were outraged. The university chancellor released statements declaring that the park was still university property. He said the users were trespassing. At 4:00 A.M. on May 15, 1969, 250 police officers started to build an eight-foot-high fence around the park. By 9:00 in the morning, a rally for People's Park had drawn a crowd of more than 2,000 people.

The people did not want to give up their park, and the rally quickly turned into a riot. People stormed the street.

They trampled over a line of policemen, sending 47 injured officers to the hospital. The president of the university met with the mayor and the police chief and decided that the safety of citizens could no longer be guaranteed. The university president called Reagan. He wanted Reagan to bring in the National Guard.

Reagan called 2,200 National Guard troops into Berkeley. The guardsmen had to fire gunshots to get the crowd under control. That day, known as Bloody Thursday, thirteen rioters were hospitalized with shotgun wounds. One later died. In the following days, about 1,000 people were arrested. National Guard troops stood guard over the area for more than two weeks until the situation calmed down.

Reagan sent 2,200 National Guardsmen to Berkeley to clamp down on student demonstrations in March 1969. The decision won him the approval of some Californians and the disdain of others.

Some Californians supported Reagan's tough stance. Many felt that the protesters were out of control and dangerous. Others saw Reagan's response as unnecessarily harsh. They felt that sending troops to control people was a violation of freedom.

A RUN FOR PRESIDENT

Despite the controversy, Reagan's performance in California was winning him more and more support in the Republican Party. In 1968 Republican leaders encouraged him to run for the Republican nomination for president. Reagan campaigned for a few months but bowed out when Richard Nixon defeated him in several primary elections. Although discouraged, Reagan took the loss in stride. After all, he had only served in political office for two years. "I wasn't ready to be president," he said later.

Reagan was prepared to run for another term as governor, however. He was reelected to a second four-year term in 1970.

While serving as governor, the Reagans purchased a ranch north of San Diego. They called it Tip Top Ranch. They planned to make the ranch their hideaway after Reagan left office. He could spend time riding horses and relaxing.

As governor, Reagan concentrated on three main goals: reducing taxes and government spending, finding a less costly welfare package, and supporting higher education. He made an impact on all three areas. Although he had to raise taxes the first year, Reagan kept his promise to return some of that money to the people. Over his eight years as governor, he issued tax rebates four times. Reagan also developed a program that lowered the amount of state money spent on welfare programs while still getting benefits to those in need. During his first years in office, Reagan reduced the amount of university funding by 27 percent. Once student protests declined, he increased university funds. By the end of his second term, Reagan had more than doubled the amount of university support from what it was when he took office.

In 1974 Reagan decided not to seek another term as governor of California. During Reagan's first months out of office, people from all over the county called, urging him to run for the Republican presidential nomination in 1976. Reagan seriously considered the proposal. As governor, he had experienced the satisfaction that comes with making a difference. During

the spring of 1975, Reagan thought a lot about the future of America. He came to the conclusion that a candidate does not make the decision to run for president—the people do. He decided to run for the Republican nomination.

✧ ————————

Reagan's lighthearted nature was not enough to win him the 1976 Republican nomination over the more stoic Gerald Ford (right).

Reagan campaigned against President Gerald Ford for the Republican nomination. He used his accomplishments as governor of California to build his campaign. But Reagan did not do as well as Ford in the primary elections, and Ford secured the Republican nomination. Ford's political team offered Reagan the vice presidential nomination, but Reagan refused. He was not interested in being vice president. But Reagan did pledge his full support for Ford. Despite this, Ford lost the election to Democrat Jimmy Carter.

Although Reagan had failed to win the nomination, his energetic campaign had made him a political star. By this time, Reagan was eager to win the country's highest office. "I wanted to be president," Reagan said. In another four years, he would have another chance to run.

CHAPTER EIGHT

AT WORK IN WASHINGTON

It is not my intention to do away with government. It is rather to make it work— work with us, not over us; stand by our side, not ride on our back.

—Ronald Reagan, First Inaugural Address, January 20, 1981

In the 1980 elections, Reagan won the Republican nomination. He chose George H. W. Bush as his running mate for vice president. President Jimmy Carter and Vice President Walter Mondale planned to run for a second term against Reagan and Bush.

In 1980 the United States was going through a difficult period. The country's unemployment rate was high, and the economy was suffering. High inflation was making goods more and more expensive. To make matters worse, international issues were also a major concern. In 1979 a revolution in the Middle Eastern nation of Iran led to a

new government in that country. The Iranian revolutionaries were hostile to the United States. After overthrow-
ing the old Iranian government, the revolutionaries
attacked the U.S. Embassy in Tehran, Iran. They took
sixty-six Americans hostage. By the summer of 1980,
fifty-two of the hostages were still imprisoned in Iran.
The situation made Carter look powerless to protect
American citizens.

In western Asia, the Soviet Union had invaded the country of Afghanistan in 1979. The Soviets wanted to keep the
country under Communist control. Carter had few options
for responding, and the situation made him look weak.
Many Americans felt that this made the country weak.

Reagan believed it was most important that Americans
did not lose faith in their country. He wanted to restore their
sense of strength and pride. He used
this approach in his campaign.

Despite Carter's appearance
of weakness, Reagan knew
that beating an incumbent
president, or "sitting president," would not be an easy
task. The campaign became
bitter. As the struggling
nation questioned Carter's
leadership skills, President
Carter tried to portray Reagan
as a dangerous alternative to
him. Reagan, for example,
had criticized the decline
in the U.S. armed forces.

*Reagan-Bush 1980 presidential
campaign button. The presidential
campaign was heated.*

Far apart on stage and on the issues, Reagan and Carter debate in 1980.

——————————— ✧ ———————————

He felt the military was not sufficiently funded and needed strengthening. Reagan believed a strong defense was necessary to stand up to the Soviet Union and Communism. Carter responded by personally attacking Reagan. The president called Reagan a warmonger, someone who encouraged war.

Many Americans viewed such criticisms as unfair. Reagan's tough approach was making Carter look bad. Meanwhile, Reagan remained charming and positive.

The race remained close throughout summer and into the fall. Then, in October, a week before the election, Reagan and Carter held a debate on national television. During the event, Carter appeared grave and gloomy, while Reagan looked cheerful and spoke in positive terms. Reagan finished his closing statement with a simple question to the

American people. He asked if "they thought they were better off now than they had been four years earlier?" Given the state of the U.S. economy, many citizens were not better off.

The debate was a huge success for Reagan. By the time of the election, he was a heavy favorite to win.

On Election Day, Reagan planned to go out to dinner with some old friends. He decided he would not closely follow the election results as they came in. This would be too stressful. After dinner, he and Nancy planned to drive to their campaign headquarters and wait for the results. But while Reagan was still in the shower, the phone rang. Nancy answered it and shouted above the running water that it was for him. It was Jimmy Carter. Reagan spoke to President Carter for a moment and then hung up the phone.

He turned to Nancy and said, "He conceded. He said he wanted to congratulate me." Voting would not close for another two hours, but it did not matter. Reagan had already defeated Carter. He was going to be the fortieth president of the United States, and, at age sixty-nine, the oldest president ever elected.

———————————— ✧ ————————————

President Jimmy Carter concedes the 1980 presidential election.

President Reagan gives his inaugural address, January 20, 1981. On the same day, the hostage crisis in Iran came to an end.

✧ ————————————

HOSTAGE RELEASE AND REAGANOMICS

At the time of the 1980 campaign for the presidency, the United States was in a state of economic and emotional turmoil. Reagan's campaign speeches promised that he would reduce the excessive spending and taxes of the Carter administration. In addition to economic stresses, Americans also had the Iran hostage situation on their minds and worried about the fate of the hostages overseas.

Many felt that Reagan won the 1980 presidency largely because he appealed to the resiliency of the American spirit and promised to "restore a sense of stability and confidence" by addressing the economic and hostage situations that had not been solved during Carter's presidency. The American hostages being held in Iran were released on the day of Reagan's inauguration. But the economic issues that had been plaguing the United States for so long proved to be a more difficult battle.

"It is time to reawaken this industrial giant," President Reagan said about the United States during his inaugural address on a cloudy January 20, 1981. Standing outside the

Capitol Building in Washington, D.C., Reagan looked out on tens of thousands of people crowding the Mall and the Capitol grounds. Over several decades, the United States had taken an economic downturn. The national deficit peaked at an alarming $80 billion. Taxes were up, inflation kept climbing, and productivity was dropping.

SANDRA DAY O'CONNOR

During his 1980 presidential campaign, Reagan made a promise that he would appoint a woman to the U.S. Supreme Court. This was a landmark announcement, considering that in the long history of the U.S. Supreme Court, every one of the justices had been male. True to his word, Reagan appointed Sandra Day O'Connor, a judge on the Arizona Court of Appeals, in late 1981.

O'Connor's nomination sparked a great deal of debate from Reagan's conservative supporters. They believed her stance on abortion and other issues was too liberal. While conservatives, fundamentalists, and antiabortion activists fought against O'Connor's nomination, many national women's groups applauded the president's move.

But O'Connor could not become a justice without Senate approval. After three days of hearings, the Senate voted unanimously to confirm her appointment. On September 25, 1981, O'Connor was sworn in to her position as the first female Supreme Court justice *(above)*.

Reagan had to convince Congress that his ideas to put the United States back on its feet would work. In early February 1981, Reagan addressed the nation in a television broadcast to explain his economic plans for the nation. He wanted to reduce taxes and encourage productivity in business. He also planned to reduce government spending. Reagan and his advisers believed this aspect of the plan would help control inflation. Shortly after the TV appearance, Reagan sent a bill to Congress, calling for an across-the-board 30 percent tax cut over a three-year period.

President Reagan addresses the American public on national television, explaining his plan to strengthen the U.S. economy. Critics and supporters of the president's economic program called it "Reaganomics."

Many Democratic Congress members disapproved of the bill. The country was billions of dollars in debt. Lowering the government's income by lowering taxes would only make this worse. But Reagan believed that lower taxes would help the economy. With a stronger economy, people and businesses would make more money. These increased profits would mean more taxes would be paid because the extra money would be taxed.

The economic program Reagan implemented during his presidency became known as Reaganomics. This approach to healing the economy focused on low taxes, fewer and cheaper government programs, and high military spending. Reaganomics was intended to keep inflation down. The president believed his program was the best way to rebuild America's failing economy.

Democrats wanted to take a different approach. They suggested drastic cuts to defense spending. But Reagan was determined to increase the country's defense budget. In Reagan's opinion, the armed services was one area of government that had suffered years of neglect. According to the Pentagon, the Soviet Union was spending 50 percent more on weapons each year than the United States was. Reagan believed that a Soviet Union that was stronger than the United States posed a threat to world peace. He wanted "peace through strength" for the American people.

Reversing the years of neglect would be expensive and difficult, but Reagan was determined to stand behind his words. During his campaign, Reagan had been repeatedly asked, "What if it comes down to a choice between national security and the deficit?" In response, he had answered, "I'd have to come down on the side of national defense."

Reagan believed that if businesses and investors had less tax burden, more money and jobs would "trickle down" to others. Critics, like those at left, strongly disagreed.

✧ ————————

Every time he had spoken these words, the crowds cheered. Reagan later commented, "Nobody wanted a second-class army, navy, or air force defending our country." Reagan desperately wanted a balanced budget, but not at the expense of the military. He later said, "I believed we could have a balanced budget . . . by 1984 at the latest."

Reagan's economic programs did boost parts of the economy, but at an expense to other parts. Reagan's tax cuts greatly favored the middle class and wealthy people. Meanwhile, his cuts in government spending affected welfare programs designed to help poor people. Poverty levels climbed, causing many people to become homeless. Hundreds of thousands of poor Americans slept on park benches, sidewalks, or anywhere they could find shelter. Breadlines that hadn't been seen since the Great Depression of the 1930s began opening in cities. The national debt also rose.

HONEY, I FORGOT TO DUCK

March 30, 1981, started off in the usual way for the new president. Reagan put on a brand-new blue suit. He then left the White House for the Hilton Hotel. At the Hilton, he gave a speech to the Construction Trades Council. After his speech, the president left the hotel through a side entrance. Passing through a line of photographers and TV cameras, Reagan was almost to his car when he heard a sound like three firecrackers going off. He turned and asked, "What [was] that?"

At that moment, the head of the Secret Service unit grabbed Reagan and pushed him into the waiting limousine.

Onlookers scramble as police and Secret Service agents swarm a suspected shooter after a sound like firecrackers erupted near President Reagan on March 30, 1981. Assistant to the President and White House Press Secretary James Brady lies face down in the crowd (center), *apparently injured.*

The popping Reagan heard was gunshots. Someone in the crowd had fired a gun. In the limousine, the Secret Service agent jumped on top of Reagan to protect him from further bullets. When the agent landed, Reagan felt an excruciating pain in his chest. He thought he had broken a rib.

As the limousine raced away from the hotel, Reagan tried to sit up. He was practically paralyzed with pain. He coughed up a large amount of blood. Reagan thought his broken rib had punctured a lung. He then noticed blood on his clothing. Reagan used his handkerchief to try to soak up the blood. The agent instructed the driver to rush to George Washington University Hospital. President Reagan had been shot.

By the time they reached the hospital, Reagan's handkerchief was drenched with blood, and he could barely breathe. Reagan walked into the hospital and told the nurse he was having trouble breathing. The next thing he knew, he was lying on a gurney. His new suit was being torn off of him. The bullet had missed his heart by less than an inch. It was lodged in his lung, causing it to collapse.

One of the doctors told Reagan that they would have to operate on him. Never losing his sense of humor, Reagan responded, "I hope you're a Republican."

He said, "Today, Mr. President, we're all Republicans."

When Reagan awoke hours later, Nancy was sitting beside him. "Honey," he said. "I forgot to duck." He borrowed the line from boxer Jack Dempsey. Dempsey had spoken those words to his wife after he lost the heavyweight championship to Gene Tunney in 1926.

American citizens were shocked at the attempted assassination. When Reagan got back to the White House, he had

Reagan recovers from his gunshot wound (left). *Only months later, Reagan was confronted with an air traffic controllers' strike* (group of strikers, right) *that threatened the economy and safety of U.S. skies. In a controversial move, Reagan fired the 11,500 striking controllers on August 5, 1981.*

mountains of get-well mail waiting for him. He paid special attention to any postcard or letter addressed to "Dutch." He knew these letters would be from old friends.

The shooter had been captured and arrested right away. Questioning revealed that John Hinckley Jr., a mentally disturbed young man, had tried to kill the president for personal reasons. Reagan never saw Hinckley at the hotel through the crowd of reporters. Hinckley later was found not guilty by reason of insanity and committed to a mental hospital.

ARMS REDUCTION
Back in the White House, Reagan was ready to lead the nation. Reagan, like many Americans, felt threatened by what appeared to be a large weapons buildup by the Soviet Union.

Since the end of World War II, the United States and the Soviet Union had been engaged in a dangerous arms race. Both superpowers were building large stockpiles of nuclear weapons. By the early 1960s, the two superpowers had built enough nuclear bombs to threaten the world's survival. One of these devastating weapons could destroy an entire city in minutes. Any nuclear battle between the two countries would surely result in the deaths of hundreds of millions of people—perhaps the destruction of the entire world. "No one can win a nuclear war," Reagan said.

At the same time, each superpower was working to develop ways to strike at the other through better and faster aircraft and missiles. Defense budgets were spiraling out of control. Beginning in the 1960s, the United States and the Soviet Union had engaged in discussions to limit the number of nuclear weapons they were building. For example, in 1969 the Strategic Arms Limitation Talks (SALT) began. These meetings led to the Strategic Arms Limitation Treaty, which was signed in May 1972. The treaty limited the number of missiles each side was allowed to produce. Yet both sides continued to build newer, more sophisticated missiles. The treaty lessened the strain on each country's defense budget but did little to reduce the threat of nuclear war.

"There is a myth," Reagan stated, "that arms control agreements automatically produce arms reduction." Reagan wanted to start talks that didn't just limit nuclear arms but reduced them. In June 1982, Reagan began the Strategic Arms Reduction Treaty Talks (START) with the Soviet Union. But these talks made little progress.

"STAR WARS" (SDI)

Reagan's ultimate dream was to rid the world of nuclear weapons. But he knew that such a process would be long and difficult. He decided the best route would be to create a defense against the missiles that delivered nuclear weapons.

On March 23, 1983, Reagan announced his decision to establish a research program called the Strategic Defense Initiative (SDI). The program, which became known as Star Wars, was as ambitious and as high tech as the movie after which it was nicknamed. Using space-age technology, the plan called for a system of satellites in outer space that would use laser beams to shoot down any attacking missiles that might be coming from other countries.

Reagan's plan was to build the system and then share it with all of the countries in the world. A shield would be built around the earth, making nuclear missiles obsolete.

———————————— ✧ ————————————

Reagan unveils his Strategic Defense Initiative in an address to the nation in 1983. Reagan hoped SDI would make nuclear weapons obsolete.

But the Soviets—and other nations—did not believe that the United States meant to share the technology. They thought the United States would attack them and then use SDI to prevent a counterattack. Soviet leader Mikhail Gorbachev reasoned that since the United States did not share manufacturing machinery, petroleum equipment, and farming implements with the Soviets, it would hardly be likely to share serious technology like that of SDI. "Let's be realistic and pragmatic," Gorbachev urged Reagan, "That's more reliable [than SDI]." The Soviets protested against SDI for another reason. It would be extremely expensive to develop and build. The Soviet economy was showing signs of serious strain. How could it afford an expensive new program?

GRENADA

While Reagan was making plans for his space program, the United States faced threats closer to home. Cuba, a large island nation only ninety miles off the coast of Florida, was under Communist rule. It had long been a thorn in the side of the United States. During the 1980s, Cuba's ruler, Fidel Castro, caused tensions to rise even further between Cuba and the United States. Castro moved Cuban troops onto the small island of Grenada in the West Indies. On October 13, 1983, Communist forces led the Grenadian army to seize power in Grenada. The bloody takeover caused concern in the United States and its nearby allies in Central America and in the Caribbean region. These allies worried that Castro and other Communist armies might try to expand Communism into other countries in the region. Also, about one thousand Americans were living in Grenada at the time.

After a sleepless night of deliberation, President Reagan makes the call to send U.S. troops into Grenada on October 25, 1983.

On October 22, 1983, the Organization of Eastern Caribbean States requested U.S. military assistance to restore stability to Grenada. At 5:15 in the morning, Reagan was informed of the situation. On October 25, he directed U.S. troops to invade Grenada. Greatly outnumbered, most of the Communist-controlled Grenadian army and armed Cubans surrendered. Others fled into the mountains. U.S. troops continued to hunt down stragglers for several days. By December, U.S. forces had left Grenada, and a pro-American government was set up on the island.

Reagan's first term had been eventful. Many Americans, at first uncertain of Reagan's new style of leadership, were firmly behind him by the end of his first term in office. He had ended the soaring inflation of prices that had hurt Jimmy Carter's presidency. He had toughened the nation's stance against its enemies, and he had become a national hero when he took an assassin's bullet in Washington.

CHAPTER NINE

ANOTHER FOUR YEARS

After all our hard-won victories earned through the patience and courage of every citizen, we cannot, must not, and will not turn back. We will finish our job. How could we do less? We're Americans.

—Ronald Reagan, State of the Union Address, 1988

In 1984 Reagan ran for a second term as president, winning in a landslide against Walter Mondale, Jimmy Carter's former vice president. At age 73, Reagan was ready to serve America for another four years.

SUMMITS WITH GORBACHEV

During the first five years of Reagan's presidency, the Soviet Union went through four leaders. Leonid Brezhnev died in 1982 and was replaced by Yuri Andropov. Andropov died in 1984. Konstantin Chernenko became the next leader, but he died in 1985. Reagan wanted to negotiate with the

Ronald Reagan and Mikhail Gorbachev meet in Geneva, Switzerland, to negotiate a nuclear arms treaty in 1985.

Soviets, but he found this very difficult when the leaders kept changing.

In 1985 Mikhail Gorbachev became the new leader of the Soviet Union. Reagan's relations with the first three leaders had been cold. Little compromising took place at summit meetings. But Gorbachev was hailed as a skillful negotiator.

Reagan and Gorbachev first met during the winter of 1985 in Geneva, Switzerland. At the summit meeting, Reagan said to Gorbachev, "What a unique position we are in. Here we are, two men born in obscure rural hamlets in the middle of our respective countries, and now, together, we can [stop] a World War III... and don't we owe this to mankind?" The two men sat beside a roaring fire and discussed their hopes for the future. During their fireside chat, the two men developed a friendly relationship.

The first summit meeting did not end with leaps and bounds toward world peace, but it ended with a better understanding between the two leaders. To Reagan, this was the first step toward peace. When he gave his report to the House of Representatives, they responded with loud cheering and stomping. Reagan wrote in his diary, "I haven't gotten such a reception since I was shot."

Afterward, Reagan and Gorbachev exchanged a series of personally written letters. They next met in person in Reykjavik, Iceland, during the summer of 1986. This summit got off to a strong start as Gorbachev told Reagan he was prepared to drastically reduce his arsenal of nuclear weapons. Gorbachev told Reagan that he would only do this if Reagan gave up his SDI plan. Gorbachev, it became clear, did not believe Reagan's promise to share the missile-defense system with the Soviets. This mistrust angered Reagan, and he walked out of the meeting.

TALKS BRING RESULTS

Reagan and Gorbachev met for a third time in Washington, D.C., in December 1987. During this meeting, Gorbachev agreed to reduce the number of Soviet nuclear weapons, even if Reagan continued with the SDI research. Reagan also agreed to reduce the number of American nuclear weapons. This meeting marked the greatest accomplishment in Soviet and American relations in more than forty years. Two nations that had hated and feared one another were finally showing signs of friendship and trust. They were actually cooperating with one another to make the world a safer place.

During a visit to Moscow in 1988, Reagan gave a speech on democracy to students at Moscow State University.

Amid news of faltering arms talks with the Soviet Union, Reagan had the sad duty of informing the nation of the Space Shuttle Challenger *disaster* (left) *in January 1986. Reagan had better news for the nation after he and Gorbachev signed a historic nuclear arms limitation treaty in 1987* (right).

When he finished, the students gave him a standing ovation. By the end of his second term, Reagan called Gorbachev his friend. Reagan hoped his new relationship with the Soviet Union would be a start in negotiations that his successors could follow.

IRAN-CONTRA SCANDAL

Although Reagan made strides in global negotiations, his office faced scandal. It is the policy of the United States and many other governments not to negotiate with terrorists. The reason for this is simple. To discuss issues with terrorists, let alone give them what they want, encourages people to use terrorism and violence to achieve their goals. This was the publicly stated policy of the Reagan administration.

Yet in private, government officials working under Reagan did negotiate with terrorists. In fact, Reagan officials not only negotiated with terrorists, they sold weapons to them. Worse yet, these officials used the money from these sales to violate laws of the United States. When these actions were discovered, they created a whirlwind of public outrage. The events became known as the Iran-Contra scandal.

In the mid-1980s, U.S. government officials had secretly negotiated with members of the Iranian government to help free seven American hostages held in the Middle Eastern nation of Lebanon. U.S. officials believed the Iranians would be able to convince the Lebanese terrorists to release the hostages. Yet the U.S. government considered Iranian leaders at the time to be terrorists. Iran had itself taken American hostages in 1979. The deal to free the hostages in Lebanon included selling weapons to the Iranian government.

Meanwhile, U.S. government officials secretly used the money from the arms sales to aid a Central American group known as the contras. The contras were revolutionary fighters working to overthrow the Communist government of the nation of Nicaragua. Strongly anti-Communist, the Reagan administration wanted to see Nicaragua's Communist leaders removed from power.

Yet in 1984, Congress had passed a law forbidding the United States from supporting the contras. Congress wanted to keep the United States from getting into another costly war like the one in Vietnam. So the people involved in funneling money to the contras, including Lieutenant Colonel Oliver North (a member of Reagan's National Security Council), tried to keep these actions a secret.

Eventually, the illegal activities were revealed, and Congress set up televised investigating committees. The Iran-Contra scandal dominated the nation's headlines. Although North implicated Reagan in the scandal, the president denied any knowledge of the "arms-for-hostages" swap, as it was called. Several members of Reagan's staff went before the U.S. Congress to answer questions on the matter. But these men, including Reagan's national security adviser, John Poindexter, contradicted North's testimony by swearing that Reagan had never been involved in the scandal.

Increasing public scrutiny of the Iran-Contra scandal led Reagan to admit his administration's involvement (but not his own) in the scandal during a nationally televised address (above) on March 4, 1987.

LIEUTENANT COLONEL OLIVER NORTH

News of the Iran-Contra scandal broke in November 1986, when reports in Lebanese newspapers made the illegal arms deals public. Soon headlines on the Iran-Contra deal were all over U.S. papers. Congressional committees were formed to conduct televised hearings investigating the affair.

Lieutenant Colonel Oliver North *(below)*, a member of President Reagan's National Security Council, was linked to the arms deals and was summoned to testify in the Iran-Contra hearings. During the hearings, North testified that he believed Reagan was aware of the Iran-Contra affair and its cover-up. Both the president and the vice president argued otherwise, stating that they had not known of the dealings. Furthermore, Reagan's national security adviser, Admiral John Poindexter, who had worked extensively with North, stated that he had been in charge of the cover-up and deliberately withheld information from the president. No evidence was found to directly link Reagan to the illegal activities, though some believe he had participated indirectly in the affair by encouraging support of the contras.

The hearings led to a criminal trial for North and others. In May 1989, North was convicted of altering and destroying documents, accepting an illegal payment, and withholding information from Congress. These convictions were dismissed in September 1991, because it was believed that the jury in the 1989 trial had been negatively influenced by North's televised Congressional testimony.

This political artwork criticizes President Reagan for his apparent connection to the Iran-Contra scandal. Though the president was cleared of any wrongdoing in the scandal, many believed that he must have known about the illegal activities.
——————————— ✧

In the end, the illegal activities were never directly linked to the president. But the fact that such a thing was going on under his watch made Reagan look bad in the eyes of the public. Either he knew about the illegal activity and was lying, or he was totally out of touch with what was going on in his administration. Either way, many wondered how much control Reagan had over his staff.

The Iran-Contra scandal also earned Reagan a nickname: the Teflon President. Like Teflon (the coating used on frying pans to keep food from sticking), nothing negative ever seemed to stick to Reagan.

CHAPTER TEN

AFTER THE WHITE HOUSE

*They called it the Reagan revolution. Well, I'll
accept that, but for me it always seemed more
like the great rediscovery, a rediscovery of our
values and our common sense.*
—Ronald Reagan, Farewell Address, 1989

The Twenty-second Amendment of the U.S. Constitution
only allows a person to be elected president for two terms.
Had Reagan been willing and able to run, presidential-
approval polls indicated that the likelihood of his winning a
third term was good. Instead, Vice President George H. W.
Bush won the Republican nomination in 1988. Bush went
on to win the presidential election.

The day before he was to leave the White House,
Reagan got up earlier than usual. He walked into the Oval
Office one last time. On the desk, Reagan had always kept
a small pad of paper with the heading "Don't Let the
Turkeys Get You Down." This was typical Reagan style,

using humor to deal with his problems. On the pad, Reagan wrote a note to President George Bush. It read:

"You'll have moments when you want to use this particular stationery. Well, go for it. George, I treasure the memories we share and wish you all the very best. You'll be in my prayers. God bless you and Barbara. I'll miss our Thursday lunches."

All the members of Reagan's staff had submitted their resignations the day before, on January 19, 1989. He didn't expect anyone to come into the Oval Office that morning. But Chief of Staff Ken Duberstein and National Security Adviser Colin Powell showed up at the regular meeting time. As they sat in the office, Powell said, "Mr. President, the world is quiet today." The group posed for one last photo and left the Oval Office.

President Reagan with staff and a film crew just moments before his farewell address to the nation in January 1989

98 ———————— R O N A L D   R E A G A N ———————— ✧

On January 20, 1989, George H. W. Bush was inaugu-
rated as president. After the ceremonies, Reagan and Nancy
climbed aboard a helicopter. The pilot circled the White
House. Referring to the large presidential home, Reagan
humorously understated the matter by saying to Nancy,
"Look, honey, there's our little bungalow." The couple then
flew home to California.

Back in California, the Reagans arrived at their new
house in Bel Air. Boxes lined the floor, waiting to be

unpacked. Many people
often feel nervous and
tense during times of
great change in their lives.
For Reagan, however, per-
haps because of his confidence, changing from one
phase of life to the next
was never a problem.

✧ ————————————

*President and Nancy Reagan
leave the White House and
board the presidential helicopter
for the airport on January 20,
1989. On the same day,
Reagan's former vice president,
George H. W. Bush, was sworn
in as president.*

Reagan and Nancy read cards from well-wishers while at the Mayo Medical Center in Rochester, Minnesota, following brain surgery in September 1989.

BATTLING ALZHEIMER'S DISEASE

In July 1989, Reagan and Nancy visited friends at a ranch in Mexico. While out horseback riding at the ranch, Reagan was thrown from his horse. He hit his head hard on the ground. Reagan was immediately flown to a hospital in Tucson, Arizona.

Shortly after they returned home, Reagan had an X ray of his skull. The test showed that Reagan had a concussion and had to be operated on right away. The operation was performed at the world-renowned Mayo Medical Center in Minnesota.

In 1990 Reagan's autobiography, *An American Life,* was published. Admirers and critics made the book a bestseller.

During one of his final public appearances, Reagan posed with (from left to right) Presidents Gerald Ford, Richard Nixon, George H. W. Bush, and Jimmy Carter in 1991.

In 1994 Reagan was diagnosed with Alzheimer's, a disease that causes progressive loss of memory, confusion, and, ultimately, death. Doctors believe the blow to his head quickened the onset of the disease. Reagan and Nancy had to decide if they should keep the news private or reveal it to the public. After much thought, they decided that they had always been open with the American people about their physical struggles in the past. This was no different.

Reagan wrote a letter to the American people. In his letter he stated, "At the moment I feel just fine. I intend to live the remainder of the years God gives me on this earth doing the things I have always done. I will continue to share life's journey with my beloved Nancy and my family."

Since the late 1990s, the Reagans have remained out of the public eye, choosing to cope with the president's disease in private with family. While the illness continues to progress, President Reagan and Nancy live life together as fully as possible.

REAGAN'S LEGACY

Looking back on his life as an athlete, an actor, and a politician, Ronald Reagan was a man of great character. Because of that character, he became a strong leader. When Reagan entered the White House, the country was plagued with self-doubt. But Reagan's confidence and strength helped the United States become a stronger and more confident nation.

✧ ────────────

President Ronald Reagan salutes the people and the nation that he loves and admires.

*East Germans meet West Germans for the first time in years during the
dismantling of the Berlin wall in 1989. Pressure from the Reagan
administration on the Soviet Union and the Eastern bloc helped East Germans
break away from Soviet control and reunite with West Germany.*

Reagan's "peace through strength" philosophy proved
very successful. He strengthened the U.S. military. His
tough stance against the Soviet Union backed Gorbachev
into a corner. The Soviet economy could not keep up the
arms race. Shortly before Reagan left office, Gorbachev
announced that the Soviet Union would make huge
reductions to its military.

The years after Reagan left office saw extraordinary
changes. The Soviet Union, the most powerful Communist
nation, began to come apart at the seams. In 1989 the
countries under Soviet control began to demand their
independence. One by one, Soviet-dominated Eastern

European countries, such as Poland, Hungary, and Romania, broke free. Each country held elections and began new paths to freedom.

At the same time, the separate states within the Soviet Union began to demand independence. Soviet states, including Ukraine, Lithuania, Latvia, Kazakhstan, and Uzbekistan, claimed their right to be free and independent states. The changes occurred at breathtaking speed. By the end of 1991, the Soviet Union had broken apart and ceased to exist. The Cold War ended peacefully.

As he himself might have put it, Ronald Reagan was a man who "stuck to his guns." No matter what the scandal or how much pressure was put upon him, he never drifted away from the principles, people, and nation in which he believed. It is for that faith that he will be best remembered.

TIMELINE

1911 Ronald Reagan is born on February 6 in Tampico, Illinois. His parents are Nelle and John Edward "Jack" Reagan. He has one older brother, John Neil. He is called Dutch by his family and friends.

1920 The Reagan family moves to Dixon, Illinois, about 90 miles west of Chicago.

1924 Reagan enters Dixon's Northside High School. He wants to play football but does not make the team. He is much smaller than the other players.

1926 Reagan takes a job as a lifeguard at Lowell Park on the Rock River. During his lifeguard career, Reagan saved seventy-seven people from drowning.

1928 Reagan enrolls at Eureka College. He has only enough money saved for one year of study.

1929 Reagan returns to Eureka College on a scholarship. During college, he played football, became captain of the swim team, and served as student body president. The Great Depression begins. People across the United States experience great economic hardships. Many businesses and banks close, and thousands of people lose their jobs.

1932 Reagan graduates from Eureka with majors in economics and sociology. He begins working as a sports announcer at WOC radio in Davenport, Iowa.

1933 Reagan takes a job as a full-time sports broadcaster at WHO radio station in Des Moines, Iowa.

1937 Reagan joins the cavalry. He becomes a second lieutenant in the Army Officers Reserve Corps. He meets with Hollywood agent Bill Meiklejohn while in California on assignment with WHO Radio. He signs a contract with Warner Brothers. Months later, Reagan stars in his first film—*Love Is on the Air.*

1940   Reagan marries actress Jane Wyman on January 26. He stars as the Gipper in *Knute Rockne, All American.* The Gipper becomes Reagan's most remembered role.

1941   Wyman and Reagan's daughter Maureen is born on January 4. Japanese planes bomb Pearl Harbor in Hawaii on December 7. The United States enters World War II by declaring war against Japan on December 8. Reagan is called into active service and is assigned to the Motion Picture Army Unit.

1945   Japan surrenders in September, bringing an end to World War II. Reagan and Wyman adopt Michael Edward.

1947   Reagan is elected president of the Screen Actors Guild. He works on important legal battles affecting the film industry.

1948   Reagan and Wyman divorce. Wyman is granted custody of their two children, and Reagan is granted visitation rights.

1952   Reagan marries actress Nancy Davis on March 4. Their daughter Patricia is born on October 22.

1954   Reagan accepts a job as host of the *General Electric Theater* television program. He tours GE plants to speak to employees.

1958   Nancy gives birth to Ronald Prescott on May 28.

1962   Reagan resigns from the Democratic Party, becoming a registered member of the Republican Party. His mother, Nelle, dies of Alzheimer's disease.

1965   The United States begins fighting in the Vietnam War. Reagan's autobiography *Where's the Rest of Me?* is published.

1966   Reagan runs against incumbent Pat Brown for governor of California. Reagan defeats Brown with 58 percent of the votes.

1969   Riots take place at People's Park near the Berkeley campus on May 15, in what came to be called Bloody Thursday.

1976 Reagan runs for the Republican nomination for president, but he is defeated by Gerald Ford.

1980 Reagan runs for president against Jimmy Carter and is elected fortieth president of the United States.

1981 Reagan announces his program for economic recovery. He is shot by John Hinckley Jr. on March 30. Later that year, Reagan fires striking air traffic controllers, claiming the controversial action is to maintain public safety and the economy.

1983 Five thousand U.S. troops invade Grenada on October 25.

1984 Reagan runs for a second term as president. He defeats Democrat Walter Mondale. At age 73, Reagan becomes the oldest person to be elected president.

1985 On November 17, Reagan arrives in Geneva, Switzerland, for a summit meeting with Mikhail Gorbachev.

1986 U.S. space shuttle *Challenger* explodes after seventy-three seconds of flight on January 28. The explosion kills six astronauts and one civilian. An investigation begins on the Iran-Contra scandal.

1988 Reagan travels to Moscow for a final summit with Gorbachev. Vice President George H. W. Bush is elected the forty-first president of the United States.

1989 Reagan and Nancy return home to California.

1990 Reagan's autobiography, *An American Life,* is published.

1991 The Soviet Union dissolves, and all former Soviet republics gain independence.

1994 Reagan is diagnosed with Alzheimer's disease. Nancy and Reagan decide to be open with the public and announce his condition to the American public.

2001 Reagan's daughter Maureen dies on August 8, after battling cancer.

Source Notes

7 Edmund Morris, *Dutch: A Memoir of Ronald Reagan* (New York: Random House, 1999), 62.

9 J. H. Cardigan, *Ronald Reagan: A Remarkable Life* (Kansas City, MO: Ariel Books, 1995), 25.

9 Ronald Reagan, *An American Life* (New York: Simon & Schuster, 1990), 21.

10 Ronald Reagan, with Richard G. Hubler, *Where's the Rest of Me?* (1965, reprint; New York: Karz Publishers, 1981), 9.

11 Reagan, *An American Life,* 21.

16 Ibid., 15.

17 Ibid., 16.

22 Reagan and Hubler, *Where's the Rest of Me?,* 21.

23 Ibid., 40.

25 Reagan, *An American Life,* 48.

26 Ibid., 50.

28 Ibid., 59.

29 Ibid., 64.

29 Ibid., 65.

34 Ibid., 86.

36 Reagan and Hubler, *Where's the Rest of Me?,* 72.

36 Ibid., 73.

36 Reagan, *An American Life,* 81.

37 Ibid.

38 Ibid., 86.

46 Ibid., 135.

51 Ibid. 121.

55 Ibid., 128.

57 Reagan, *An American Life,* 136.

59 Reagan, *An American Life,* 147.

59 Ibid., 151.

60 Ibid.

68 Lou Cannon, *Ronald Reagan* (New York: Public Affairs Book, 2001), 57.

71 Reagan, *An American Life,* 209.

72 Ronald Reagan, "Ronald Reagan, 1981 Inaugural Address," *Presidential Inaugurations,* July 15, 2003, <http://memory.loc.gov/ammem/pihtml/pi058. html> (July 15, 2003).

75 Reagan, *An American Life,* 221.

75 Reagan, *An American Life,* 222.

76 Lou Cannon, *President Reagan: The Role of a Lifetime* (New York: Simon & Schuster, 1991), 21, 109.

76 William E. Pemberton, *Exit with Honor: The Life and Presidency of Ronald Reagan* (New York: M. E. Sharpe, 1997), 102–104.

79 Ibid., 235.

80 Ibid.

80 Ibid.

81 Ibid., 258.

82 Ibid., 261.

82 Ibid., 260.

84 Ibid., 549.

84 Ibid., 550.

86 Cannon, *President Reagan: The Role of a Lifetime,* 281, 317–318, 326, 327, 741–742.

86 "Reagan-Gorbachev Transcripts," *CNN Interactive,* June 24, 2003, <http://www.cnn.com/SPECIALS/cold.war/episodes/22/documents/reykjavik> (June 24, 2003).

89 Peggy Noonan, *When Character Was King: A Story of Ronald Reagan* (New York: Viking, 2001), 290.

90 Reagan, *An American Life,* 641.

97 Ibid., 722.

97 Ibid.

98 Nancy Reagan, *I Love You, Ronnie* (New York: Random House, 2000) 173.

100 Ibid., 188.

Selected Bibliography

Anderson, Martin. *Revolution: The Reagan Legacy.* Stanford, CA: Hoover Institution Press, 1991.

Barrett, Lawrence I. *Gambling with History: Ronald Reagan in the White House.* Garden City, NY: Doubleday, 1983.

Berman, Larry, ed. *Looking Back on the Reagan Presidency.* Baltimore: The Johns Hopkins University Press, 1990.

Cannon, Lou. *President Reagan: The Role of a Lifetime.* New York: Simon & Schuster, 1991.

————. *Ronald Reagan.* New York: Public Affairs Book, 2001.

Cardigan, J. H. *Ronald Reagan: A Remarkable Life.* Kansas City, MO: Ariel Books, 1995.

D'Souza, Dinesh. *Ronald Reagan: How an Ordinary Man Became an Extraordinary Leader.* New York: The Free Press, 1997.

Hannaford, Peter. *The Reagans: A Political Portrait.* New York: Coward-McCann, 1983.

Kent, Zachary. *Ronald Reagan: Fortieth President of the United States.* Chicago: Children's Press, 1989.

Levy, Peter B. *Encyclopedia of the Reagan-Bush Years.* Westport, CT: Greenwood Press, 1996.

Morris, Edmund. *Dutch: A Memoir of Ronald Reagan.* New York: Random House, 1999.

Noonan, Peggy. *When Character Was King: A Story of Ronald Reagan.* New York: Viking, 2001.

Pemberton, William E. *Exit with Honor: The Life and Presidency of Ronald Reagan.* New York: M. E. Sharpe, 1997.

Reagan, Nancy. *I Love You, Ronnie.* New York: Random House, 2000.

Reagan, Ronald. *An American Life.* New York: Simon & Schuster, 1990.

————. "Ronald Reagan, 1981 Inaugural Address." *Presidential Inaugurations.* July 15, 2003. <http://memory.loc.gov/ammem/pihtml/pi058.html> (July 15, 2003).

Reagan, Ronald, with Richard G. Hubler. *Where's the Rest of Me?* 1965. Reprint, New York: Karz Publishers, 1981.

"The Reagan Children," *The American Experience: Reagan,* June 24, 2003, <http://www.pbs.org/wgbh/amex/reagan/peopleevents/pande05.html> (June 24, 2003).

"Reagan-Gorbachev Transcripts," *CNN Interactive,* June 24, 2003, <http://www.cnn.com/SPECIALS/cold.war/episodes/22/documents/reykjavik> (June 24, 2003).

Ritter, Kurt, and David Henry. *Ronald Reagan: The Great Communicator.* New York: Greenwood Press, 1992.

Ryan, Frederick J. Jr., ed. *Ronald Reagan: The Great Communicator.* New York: HarperCollins Publishers, 2001.

Strober, Deborah H., and Gerald S. Strober. *Reagan: The Man and His Presidency.* Boston: Houghton Mifflin, 1998.

Wills, Garry. *Reagan's America: Innocents at Home.* New York: Doubleday, 1987.

FURTHER READING AND WEBSITES

Gherman, Beverly. *Jimmy Carter.* Minneapolis: Lerner Publications Company, 2004.

Head, Tom. *Mikhail Gorbachev.* San Diego: Greenhaven Press, 2003.

Márquez, Herón. *Russia in Pictures.* Minneapolis: Lerner Publications Company, 2004.

Orr, Tamra. *Ronald Reagan.* Philadelphia: Mason Crest Publishers, 2003.

Ronald W. Reagan Presidential Library and Museum. <http://www.reaganlibrary.net>. This official website of the Reagan Library chronicles the life and politics of Ronald Reagan.

Williams, Jean Kinney. *Ronald W. Reagan.* Minneapolis: Compass Point Books, 2003.

INDEX

ABOUT THE AUTHOR

Michael Benson, from Rochester, New York, graduated from Hofstra University with a major in communications arts. In 1987 he married Lisa Grasso, an attorney. They have two children, Tekla, 13, and Matthew, 7. They reside in Brooklyn, New York.

Benson is the former editor of *The Military Technical Journal* and the author of more than 30 books, including biographies of Bill Clinton, Gloria Estefan, and Malcolm X.

———————— ❖ ————————

PHOTO ACKNOWLEDGMENTS

The images in this book are used with the permission of: courtesy of the White House, pp. 1, 2, 7, 9, 17, 23, 34, 46, 58, 72, 88, 96; courtesy of the Ronald Reagan Library, pp. 6, 10, 11, 14, 19, 20, 24, 26, 30, 41, 44, 52, 53, 54, 77, 78, 81, 83 (left), 85, 89, 93, 97, 98, 101; *Chicago Daily News* negatives collection, Chicago Historical Society (DN-0008192), p. 12; Library of Congress, pp. 13, 32; Ronald Reagan Home Preservation Foundation, Dixon Illinois, p. 18; © Bettmann/CORBIS, pp. 27, 35, 37, 38, 39, 42, 50, 60, 61, 65, 66, 68, 74, 83 (right), 87, 94; National Baseball Library and Archive, Cooperstown, New York, p. 31; © John Springer Collection/CORBIS, p. 40; © Hulton| Archive by Getty Images, p. 47; Hollywood Book and Poster, p. 51; National Archives, p. 64; © Wally McNamee/CORBIS, pp. 70, 80; © Todd Strand/Independent Picture Service, p. 73; © CORBIS, p. 75; Bill Fitz-Patrick/the White House, p. 76; NASA, p. 91 (left); Parker Penn USA Limited, p. 91 (right); © Henry Diltz/ CORBIS, p. 95; © Dalen Merle/CORBIS SYGMA, p. 99; courtesy of the George H. W. Bush Presidential Library, p. 100; German Information Center, p. 102.

Cover photo: Hollywood Book and Poster